# Life Cycles of a Dozen Diverse Creatures

## PAUL FLEISHER

The Millbrook Press
Brookfield, Connecticut

Photographs courtesy and © Superstock: pp. 4-5; Animals, Animals: pp. 6 (Breck P. Kent), 7 (Patti Murray), 14-15 (Oxford Scientific Films), 17 (Oxford Scientific Films), 20, 22-23 (Donald Specker), 28-29 (G.L. Kooyman), 31 (Doug Allan, Oxford Scientific Films), 35 (Zig Leszczynski), 44-45 (Patti Murray), 47 (J.H. Robinson), 48 (Patti Murray), 50-51 (Lloyd Beesley), 53 (L.L. Rue III), 56-57 (Zig Leszczynski); Photo Researchers: pp. 10-11 (Gregory G. Dimijian), 18-19 (M.I. Walker), 39 (Gregory Ochocki), 59 (Paul A. Zahl), 60-61 (F. Stuart Westmorland), 66-67; Milford Laboratory, National Marine Fisheries Service, NOAA: p. 12; Phototake: pp. 25, 68; Frans Lanting, Minden Pictures: p. 33; Biological Photo Service: pp. 36-37 (David J. Wrobel); Bruce Coleman: pp. 40-41 (E.R. Degginger), 42 (E.R. Degginger), 54 (L.L. Rue III); Natalie B. Fobes: pp. 62, 63.

Library of Congress Cataloging-in-Publication Data
Fleisher, Paul.
Life cycles of a dozen diverse creatures / by Paul Fleisher.
p.   cm.
Includes bibliographical references and index.
Summary: Compares and contrasts the life cycles of twelve animals including the oppossum, bullfrog, and jellyfish.
ISBN 0-7613-0000-7 (lib. bdg.)
1. Animal life cycles—Juvenile literature. [1. Animal life cycles.] I. Title.
QH501.F56   1996
591.3—dc20   95-52717   CIP   AC

Published by The Millbrook Press, Inc.
2 Old New Milford Road
Brookfield, Connecticut 06804

*To Horace and Willette Sims:*
*Thanks for generously welcoming me*
*into your family — P.F.*

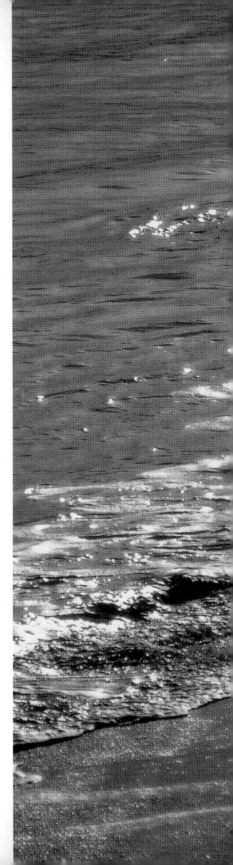

**H**uman beings are born into small family groups. Our parents care for us during childhood, while we grow and learn the skills we need to take care of ourselves. Later, as adults, many of us find partners of the opposite sex and start families of our own. Then the whole process starts again. Finally, after many years each one of us must die. We mark many of the turning points in this journey with special ceremonies: birthdays, confirmations, *bar mitzvahs*, weddings, and funerals.

The human life cycle seems completely normal to us. But it's not as ordinary as you might think. The life cycles of other living things can be very different.

A life cycle is the series of stages that any organism, or living thing, passes through as it is born, grows, reproduces, and eventually dies.

# What Is a Life Cycle?

There are millions of different species, or kinds, of plants, animals, fungi, bacteria, and other creatures living on earth. And each species has a certain way of living, growing, and reproducing. That pattern happens again and again, generation after generation, as offspring go through the same stages that their parents and grandparents did.

*The black swallowtail begins life as a caterpillar. . .*

We may think that some of the life cycles we find among the world's creatures are strange or unusual. But to each particular species, its life cycle is completely normal.

For example, certain insects hatch as small wormlike creatures we call caterpillars. A caterpillar creeps from leaf to leaf, eating as it goes. Later it wraps itself into a cocoon and changes into a creature with a totally different appearance. When it crawls out of its cocoon after several weeks, this same insect has a thinner body, delicate, colorful wings, long legs, and a long, curled tongue. The young caterpillar has become an adult butterfly. Two butterflies then mate, and the female lays eggs to begin the cycle again.

Think how different a butterfly's life cycle is from a human's! Both start as fertilized eggs and end as reproducing adults. But the steps in between are completely different. When you look at it from a butterfly's point of view, the human life cycle doesn't seem so ordinary after all.

And that's not the end of the story. The life cycles of a salmon, or an oyster, or an earthworm are all very different from one another. And each is also very different from our own.

In this book, you'll read about the life cycles of a dozen animals living on our planet. Each has its own unique way to grow and reproduce. Before we begin, let's learn

. . .and is transformed into an adult black swallowtail butterfly.

a few words that will help us understand the life cycles we are going to examine.

Reproduction is the process by which organisms make more members of their species. Living things must reproduce if their kind is to continue. Offspring are the new creatures that are created by reproduction. The creatures that produce the offspring are called parents.

Organisms have two main methods of reproducing. These are known as sexual reproduction and asexual reproduction. When an organism reproduces sexually, special reproductive cells divide in half. In males, these become sperm cells. In females, they become egg cells. Sperm cells are microscopically small, and are able to swim from place to place. Egg cells are much larger, often large enough to be seen without a magnifying lens. They don't usually move on their own. In some species, one individual can produce both sperm and eggs. In others—like humans—an individual produces one or the other, but not both.

Neither sperm nor egg is complete by itself. In most cases, one can't grow without the other. To produce a new organism, a sperm and an egg cell must join together. When this happens, we say that the egg has been fertilized. Once an egg is fertilized, it can begin to grow. In its early stages of growth, it is usually known as an embryo. After the egg hatches, the young creature is called a juvenile. An adult is an organism that has matured enough to produce offspring of its own.

In many animals, the juvenile form is known as a larva. Larvae (plural) often look very different from their adult parents. For example, caterpillars are larvae. They look nothing like their butterfly or moth parents. Larvae themselves may go through several different stages. In insects each of these stages is called an instar.

After a larva has grown enough, it changes into its adult form. This change is called metamorphosis. In our example, when a caterpillar goes through metamorphosis, it changes into an adult butterfly. During the time it is changing, a larva may go through a resting stage. It is then called a pupa.

Many animals reproduce asexually as well as sexually. The prefix *a* means "without." In asexual reproduction, an organism produces offspring without making egg and sperm cells. For example, jellyfish go through an asexual stage. One individual animal attached to a shell or rock divides and produces several jellyfish.

One of the most important characteristics of life on earth is its diversity—its tremendous variety. Living things have found ways to survive in almost every habitat on earth, from the deep ocean floor, to the icy deserts of Antarctica, to the tiny spaces between grains of sand. The human life cycle is similar to the life cycle of some animals, and very different from others. But it Is no "better" or "worse" than the life cycle of butterflies or salmon or any other species.

Each life cycle described in this book is different from the others in fascinating and surprising ways. But each animal is also part of the great web of life that makes our existence on this planet possible.

*a*n oyster spends its adult life firmly attached to a solid surface like a rock or a shell. It never moves. The soft-bodied oyster lives inside a hard shell that it produces as it grows. The oyster filters tiny particles of food from the shallow salt water it lives in. An adult oyster can live for six years or more.

An oyster doesn't start its life attached to a rock. In its growth from egg to adult, this animal goes through many different changes.

An oyster begins its life as a fertilized egg floating in the warm waters of a bay or inlet. After only about ten hours, the egg hatches into a tiny larva no bigger than a speck of dust. The larva has a fringe of tiny hairlike cilia that it uses to row itself through the water. The cilia also filter tiny food particles out of the water for the larva to eat.

*Adult oysters cluster in a salt marsh
in Aransas Bay, Texas.*

# Oyster

*Crassostrea virginica*

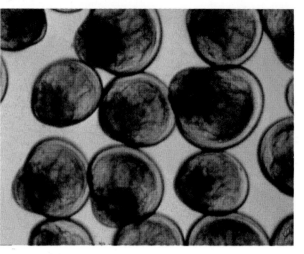

*Tiny oyster larvae, no larger than the point of a needle, attach themselves to a hard surface, and there they will grow and spend the rest of their lives.*

After just one day, the larva changes form. It metamorphoses again into a larva with a slightly different shape. The larva now looks like a tiny swimming clam. Dozens of these larvae could fit on the head of a pin.

Each larva has a thin shell and a little foot, much like a clam. It also has many cilia. It floats and swims along with the water currents, straining particles of food from the water with its cilia.

The oyster larvae float and swim in the warm waters, eating and growing. Most of the larvae end up as food for other animals that live in the bay.

After about two weeks, each surviving larva sinks to the bottom of the bay. It searches for a hard surface to attach itself to—a rock, concrete, a piece of wood, or even another oyster shell. The larva then completes its metamorphosis into adult form. It attaches its shell to the surface where it settled and never moves again. The young oyster begins growing the heavy shell that will be its home for the rest of its life.

Will the young oyster grow to maturity? It depends on how lucky it has been in choosing a home. The water must be the right depth, with enough current to keep the oyster from being covered with mud.

If there is enough food and if no predator breaks the shell and eats the oyster inside, then it will survive. By the end of the first year, the young oyster will be about 1 inch (2.5 centimeters) long.

Oysters begin reproducing when they are about a year old. Oysters spawn, or release eggs and sperm, in late spring when the water temperature reaches about 68°F (20°C). When the water gets warmer than 85°F (29°C), spawning ends.

All young adult oysters are male. During the summer mating season, they release billions of sperm into the water to fertilize the eggs of other oysters. But after their first year, something surprising happens. They change sex! Young male oysters turn into older female oysters. Once an oyster has changed from male to female, it remains female for the rest of its life.

Female oysters produce enormous numbers of eggs. The average oyster produces 15 million eggs or more in a single summer. Very few of these eggs survive to become adults, though. Most become food for other creatures in the bay.

The female oysters release the eggs into the water. When a female spawns, it opens and closes its shells, pumping out millions of eggs in about twenty minutes. Scientists believe that oysters release special chemicals that signal other oysters to begin spawning also. So, many different oysters release their sperm and egg cells into the water at the same time. This makes it more likely that eggs will meet sperm cells in the water and become fertilized. The eggs develop into tiny oyster larvae, starting the life cycle all over again.

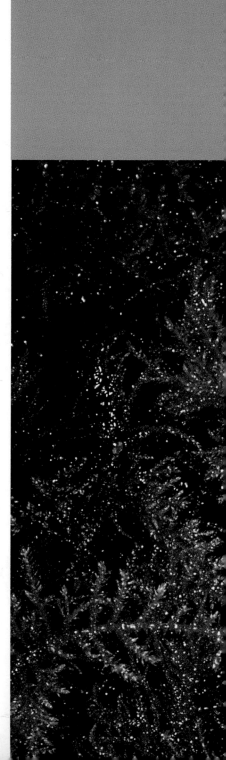

*e*arthworms play a very important part in the web of life. Earthworms burrow through the soil, helping oxygen reach the roots of plants. They turn over the soil by bringing the earth they have eaten to the surface and leaving it as "worm castings." The dead plant and animal material they eat enriches the soil as it is digested and passes through their intestines.

When earthworms die, they themselves fertilize the soil. Under perfect conditions, an earthworm may live for ten years or more. But in the natural world, very few survive that long. Many ecosystems need a busy population of earthworms to keep plants growing strong.

Look closely at an earthworm. You'll see its body seems to be made of a series of rings, called

*An earthworm's body is made up of many segments.*
*The broad, lighter-colored band is called the clitellum.*
*The earthworm's head is at the top of the picture.*

# Earthworm

## *Lumbricus terrestris*

segments. Each segment has eight tiny bristles that the worm uses to pull itself through the soil.

An earthworm does have a head end and a tail end. It also has a dorsal (back) and a ventral (belly) side to its body. An earthworm has a broad, lighter-colored band called the clitellum near its front end. This organ plays an important part in the worm's reproductive cycle.

An earthworm starts life as a fertilized egg protected inside a small egg case—sometimes called a cocoon. Worm cocoons usually contain 4 or 5 eggs, but some may hold as many as 20. Earthworms don't go through any larval stages as they grow. After two or three weeks, the egg hatches into a small, whitish worm less than 1 inch (2.5 centimeters) long.

The young earthworm digs its own burrow and begins feeding on tiny pieces of leaves and other decaying plant matter in the soil. As it grows, the worm digs deeper into the soil. Some earthworms burrow as deep as 20 feet (6 meters) below the surface, but most worms live in the top foot (30 centimeters) of the soil.

Earthworms are mature and ready to reproduce after about three months. Every earthworm is a hermaphrodite. That means it has both male and female sex organs. But an earthworm does not fertilize its own eggs. Instead, pairs of earthworms mate. Each worm fertilizes the eggs of the other.

Earthworms mate throughout the spring and summer. Earthworms come out of their burrows to mate. They face in opposite directions, belly to belly. The worms glue themselves together with slime. Sperm swim from the male organ of each worm to a sperm-storing organ of the other. Then the worms separate.

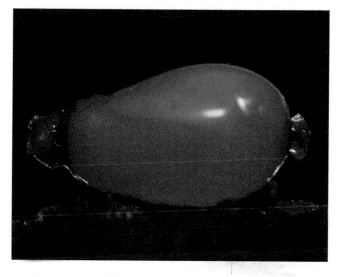

This cocoon, filled with fertilized eggs, will soon hatch a new generation of earthworms.

One or two days after they mate, each worm secretes a ring of slime from its clitellum. This slime will soon become a container for the worm's eggs. Though it is usually called a cocoon, this egg case is very different from the cocoon of a butterfly or other insect.

The ring slides over the worm's body toward its head. As it slides along, the worm releases a few eggs into the cocoon. When it slides a little further, the worm releases some of the stored sperm from its mate. The cocoon then slips off over the worm's head. As soon as it slips off, the ends of the slime ring close, sealing the eggs inside. It hardens into a protective egg case. While the cocoon is forming, the sperm fertilize the eggs. A new generation of earthworms begins.

An earthworm is able to regenerate, or regrow, parts of its body. If the front section of an earthworm is removed—by a hungry bird, for example—the worm can regrow it. The same is true if the worm loses its tail. It takes two to four weeks for the worm to regrow its lost segments.

The cut-off piece of head or tail cannot grow into a new worm. Some organisms can reproduce by dividing themselves, but earthworms do not.

*f*ill a jar with pond water and look at it closely. You'll probably see dozens of tiny specks darting and swimming in all directions. Look at those specks with a magnifying lens. You'll see that many of these tiny creatures have rounded bodies with birdlike beaks, large eyes, and branching antennae.

These tiny animals are daphnia. An adult daphnia is about the size of the period at the end of this sentence. Daphnia are sometimes called water fleas. But they are not fleas at all. They are a kind of crustacean. They are freshwater relatives of shrimp, crabs, and lobsters.

Like those other crustaceans, daphnia have stiff outer shells and many pairs of jointed legs. To feed, daphnia filter tiny food particles out of the water with hairlike filters on their legs. They use one of their two pairs of antennae to paddle themselves through the water.

*An adult daphnia.*

# Daphnia

## *Daphnia pulex*
## and other species

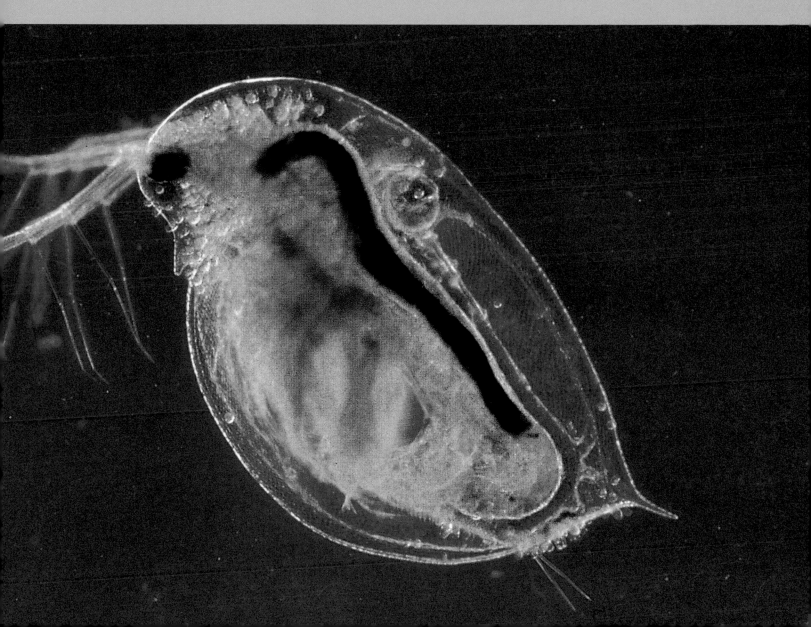

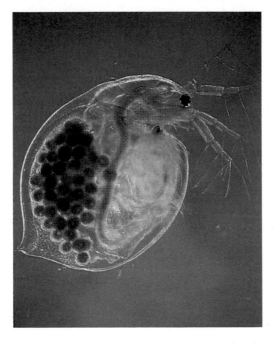

*The eggs of her all-female young are clearly visible inside the mother daphnia.*

Daphnia start life as dormant, or resting, eggs that have spent the winter months at the bottom of a pond or quiet stream. In the spring, when the water begins to warm, the eggs hatch into tiny female daphnia. The daphnia feed and grow rapidly. However, their protective shells don't grow. So daphnia must shed their shells frequently and grow larger ones.

Daphnia grow to maturity in a little more than a week. Once they begin reproducing, something surprising happens. The female daphnia produce fertile eggs on their own. These eggs don't have to be fertilized with sperm.

The mother daphnia keeps her eggs in a little pouch within her body. There, the embryos develop into young daphnia. The mother's shell is so thin that you can see the young daphnia growing inside their parent when you look through a microscope.

The young daphnia are all female, just like their mother. These daughter daphnia are actually their mother's twin sisters! They have the very same genes as their mother. This reproductive process is called parthenogenesis.

When the young daphnia have grown large enough, they leave their mother's pouch for the waters of the pond. Daphnia grow and reproduce quickly. In about a week, they too begin to produce daughters. This process continues for several generations. Each generation of mother daphnia produces more daughters, with no male daphnia at all.

Eventually, conditions in the pond become less healthy for daphnia. The pond may begin to dry up, or become so crowded that there isn't enough food. Or perhaps winter is coming and the water temperature begins to drop. Whatever the reason, something signals the daphnia to change their life cycle.

Instead of producing another generation of daughters, the female daphnia now produce both male and female offspring. When they mature, the males and females mate. The females then produce a larger and different kind of egg—a resting egg. This is the same kind of dormant egg that began the daphnia's life cycle in the early spring, many generations before.

This resting egg doesn't develop into a new daphnia right away. It is released into the water when its mother sheds her shell or dies. The resting egg sinks to the bottom of the pond. There it waits until conditions improve again.

Somehow the egg senses when the pond will again be a good home for daphnia. Only then will it hatch into new young daphnia to start the life cycle again.

*W*ild honeybees live in hollow trees or other protected locations. Many domesticated honeybees live in hives made by people. Thousands of different plants, including many crops, depend on bees to pollinate their flowers. Without bees, many plants would not be able to produce seeds and reproduce.

Unlike most insects, honeybees live in large, cooperative groups. Individual bees can't survive on their own. To understand the honeybee's life cycle, we have to examine the life cycle of the whole colony.

The life of a colony of bees revolves around one queen. A newly hatched queen flies to a special location away from her hive. There, queens and drones (male bees) from many different colonies gather. She mates with a dozen or more drones from several different hives.

*The queen honeybee is easy to see in this picture. She is much larger than the worker bees surrounding her.*

# Honeybee

## *Apis mellifera*

Honeybees mate as they fly. The drone dies a few minutes after mating. The queen stores his sperm inside a special organ in her abdomen. She will fertilize her eggs with this sperm for the rest of her life—three years or more. After mating, the queen returns to her hive. She drives away or kills any other new queens that have hatched. She then begins laying eggs, her only task for as long as she lives.

The thousands of worker bees in the colony build a comb with wax from special glands. The comb is made of hundreds of six-sided cells. The bees store honey or pollen in some of these little chambers. But they use much of the hive—called a brood comb—to raise young bees.

Workers keep the queen fed while she produces as many as 2,000 eggs a day. The queen lays one egg in each brood cell. Each egg is about 1/16 inch (1.6 millimeters) long. She fertilizes most of the eggs with the sperm she received during her mating flights. All fertilized eggs become female bees—either workers or, in special cases, a new queen. The queen also lays a few unfertilized eggs in special larger cells. These eggs become drones.

The eggs hatch into larvae in about three days. The larvae—soft, white, wormlike grubs—never leave their brood cells. Young workers—nurse bees—bring them food. For the first three days, the larvae eat royal jelly, a protein-rich food produced in the heads of the nurse bees. Then they are fed honey and pollen. The larvae are well cared for. The nurse bees visit each grub more than 1,200 times a day!

About six days after hatching, the larva begins its metamorphosis. Workers close the brood cell with wax. The larva spins a silky cocoon

*Inside the brood comb, the honeybee larvae grow and develop into pupae, then into adult honeybees.*

around itself and becomes a pupa. Inside the cocoon, the insect gradually changes into an adult bee. The metamorphosis takes about twelve days. At the end of that time, the insect chews its way out of the cell and emerges in its adult form.

Worker bees are all female. But they are sterile—they can't produce eggs. Each adult worker goes through a series of stages. At each stage the bee has a special job to do. For the first several days of its adult life, the young worker cleans and polishes the cells in the hive. This prepares the cells for the queen to lay new eggs. Then, for about a

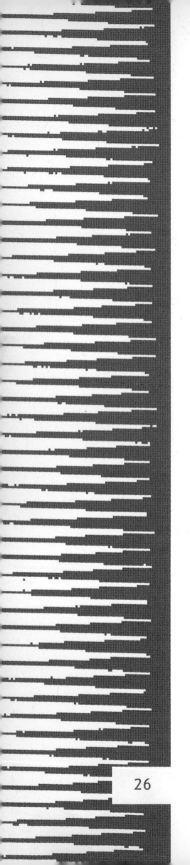

week, glands in the worker's head produce royal jelly. She spends her time as a nurse, feeding the larvae or the queen.

After a week, the worker stops producing royal jelly. Now, she makes wax from a different set of glands, in her abdomen. She uses the wax to build the hive or to close the cells of developing larvae.

After another week, the wax glands stop working. The worker then takes nectar and pollen from older workers that have been out foraging, or hunting, for food. The bees store the pollen and nectar in the honeycomb. They fan the nectar with their wings. Water evaporates from the nectar while chemicals from the bee's stomach turn it into honey.

Next, the worker spends one or two days as a guard. Guard bees stay at the entrance to the hive. They defend against attacks from other animals, and against bees from other colonies trying to steal honey.

Finally, after about three weeks inside the hive, the worker begins foraging. She may fly as far as 6 miles (10 kilometers) to gather nectar and pollen for the hive. A worker dies after about ten to twenty days of foraging. In that time, she gathers enough nectar to make about 1/4 ounce (7 grams) of honey.

Drones don't make honey or do any other work. In the fall, the workers chase all the drones from the hive. Through the winter, the bees cluster together in the center of the hive. They vibrate their wing muscles, making enough heat to keep the center of the colony warm. The cold may kill many of the workers, but enough survive to begin rebuilding the colony when spring brings new flowers and food.

Entire colonies of bees often divide and reproduce with a behavior called swarming. Swarming usually takes place in late spring or early summer, when the colony is at full strength and has lots of honey. Before swarming, the queen lays a number of eggs in especially large queen cells. Workers feed these larvae a special diet of royal jelly only. The special feeding and extra roomy cell turn the eggs into queens rather than workers. When metamorphosis is complete in about eight days, the bees will emerge from their cells as new queens.

Meanwhile, the workers in the hive become more and more excited. They seal the new queens in their cells to pupate. Then the workers drink as much honey as they can. They push the old queen to the entrance of the hive. She flies away, and about half the colony's workers leave with her in a tight swarm.

The swarm finds a temporary place to rest, usually on a tree limb. Scout bees search for a good place to build a new hive. When they find a new home—a hollow tree, for example—they lead the rest of the swarm to it. The workers begin building a new comb, and the queen starts laying eggs again.

Meanwhile, the new queens come out of their cells in the old hive. The first queen to emerge cuts open the cells of the others and stings them to death. Sometimes two or more queens emerge at the same time. If so, they fight until only one is left alive. Then the new queen goes on her mating flights, and returns to lay eggs and continue the life of the colony.

*t*he emperor penguin is one of the world's largest birds. An adult emperor can weigh up to 100 pounds (about 45 kilograms) and stands about 3 1/2 feet (1 meter) tall. Emperor penguins may live for thirty-five years or more.

Emperor penguins live on the ice shelves at the edge of Antarctica, and in the surrounding ocean. They don't fly, but they are speedy, graceful swimmers. Emperor penguins can swim as fast as 15 miles (24 kilometers) per hour. They eat fish, squid, and krill—a shrimplike crustacean. Scientists think emperor penguins may dive as deep as 1,000 feet (300 meters) below the ocean surface when they hunt.

Emperor penguins mate and raise their young on the icy shores of Antarctica. Unlike most birds, emperor penguins lay their eggs in winter. This allows the young penguins to have the full Antarctic summer to feed and grow.

*An emperor penguin keeps its chick warm while the other parent has gone to find food.*

# Emperor Penguin

*Aptenodytes forsteri*

At the beginning of the breeding season, adult penguins walk across miles of sea ice in long lines. They gather in large groups on the icy coastline of the Antarctic continent. The penguins find shelter from the cold winds beneath the barren Antarctic cliffs.

Males and females pair off. They go through a complicated courtship dance and then mate. Emperor penguins don't mate for life, but mated pairs do stay together for an entire breeding season. Like other birds, male penguins don't have a penis. The male and female press their cloacas, or reproductive openings, together. The male releases his sperm. The sperm then swim up the female's reproductive canal to fertilize her egg.

Emperor penguins don't build a nest. There is no nest-building material on Antarctica. Instead, they hold the egg on their feet. The female lays one large pear-shaped egg in late May or June—the beginning of Antarctic winter. After she produces the egg, she carefully passes it to her mate. Then she returns to the ocean to feed and regain her strength. She hasn't eaten for a month and a half, and may have lost about one third of her body weight in producing the egg.

The male holds the egg on his feet for nine weeks. A flap of skin on his belly folds over the egg, keeping it warm. Temperatures can fall below -50°F (-45°C), and Antarctic storms have fierce winds. To keep warm, thousands of male penguins huddle together through the dark Antarctic winter.

The males do not eat for two more months! They live on the fat stored in their bodies. The male penguins lose 30 to 45 percent of their body weight during the incubation period. Meanwhile, the penguin embryos grow inside their eggs. Just as the eggs start hatching, the well-fed females return. They call to find their mates. Now it's their turn to care for the babies.

The male carefully transfers the newly hatched chick to the mother's feet. She keeps it warm and protected with her flap of belly skin. She feeds her baby with fish and squid that she has stored in her crop (a digestive organ located above the stomach in most birds). By now the male has spent more than three months without eating. He returns to the sea to feed. He may have to walk across 100 miles (160 kilometers) or more of sea ice before he reaches open water.

*Around the time this egg hatches, the mother penguin will return from the sea with food for the new baby. The hungry father can then go in search of his first meal in months.*

If the female doesn't return before the egg hatches, the male can feed it for a few days with oily, protein-rich secretions from his own digestive system. This unusual food is sometimes called "penguin milk." Sometimes a female doesn't return because she has died during her feeding. If this happens, the male abandons his chick and returns to the ocean to feed. Penguins without chicks fight over lost or abandoned babies. The chicks are often killed as the adults struggle to adopt them.

After several weeks, the male returns to help the mother feed their chick.

Six weeks after it hatches, the fluffy, gray chick is too large to stay on its parents' feet. Instead, it stands in front of its parent, shielded from the cold winds. The parents take turns traveling across the ice to bring fish and squid to their growing chick.

As the chick grows larger, penguin parents spend more and more time hunting for food. While the parents are away, the chicks gather in a large group known as a crèche. These tight huddles help protect the young penguins from the cold and from predatory sea birds.

Penguin chicks grow quickly on the food from their parents' stomachs. After five months the chicks weigh about 30 pounds (14 kilograms). By December or January—the Antarctic summer—they grow their adult coat of feathers. The flocks of penguins migrate to the edge of the sea ice. As the ice melts and breaks up, the adults swim away and leave the chicks on their own. Scientists know very little about how adult emperors spend the summer months. They think that the penguins separate to hunt in the rich Antarctic waters.

The young penguins must dive into the ocean and catch their own food for the first time. Young emperor penguins look very much like their parents, but they are not yet adults. They spend their first few years at sea. Only when they are about six years old do the young emperors join the rest of the flock to mate and raise their own chicks.

These emperor penguin chicks may all look alike to us, but this parent will find
its chick among the others in the crèche, or group, by listening for its calls.

*M*ost people who swim in the bays along the Atlantic coast have met the sea nettle. The meeting is not usually a pleasant one.

The sea nettle, a kind of jellyfish, is a ghostly, whitish blob with long tentacles that trail beneath it. Sea nettles use their tentacles to paralyze and capture prey. The tentacles can sting human skin, too. The painful sting burns for an hour or more and leaves a red rash.

Sea nettles are not very well named. They can't live in fresh water, but they don't do well in seawater either. They live best in brackish water —a mixture of fresh and salt water in bays and at the mouths of rivers. In the Chesapeake Bay, sea nettles are so numerous during the summer that you often can't swim without being stung.

A jellyfish is not a fish, of course. It is a much simpler animal. It belongs to a group of animals that biologists call cnidarians. Sea

*Sea nettles are very simple creatures that spend their time floating and feeding in brackish water.*

# Sea Nettle

## *Chrysaora quinquecirrha*

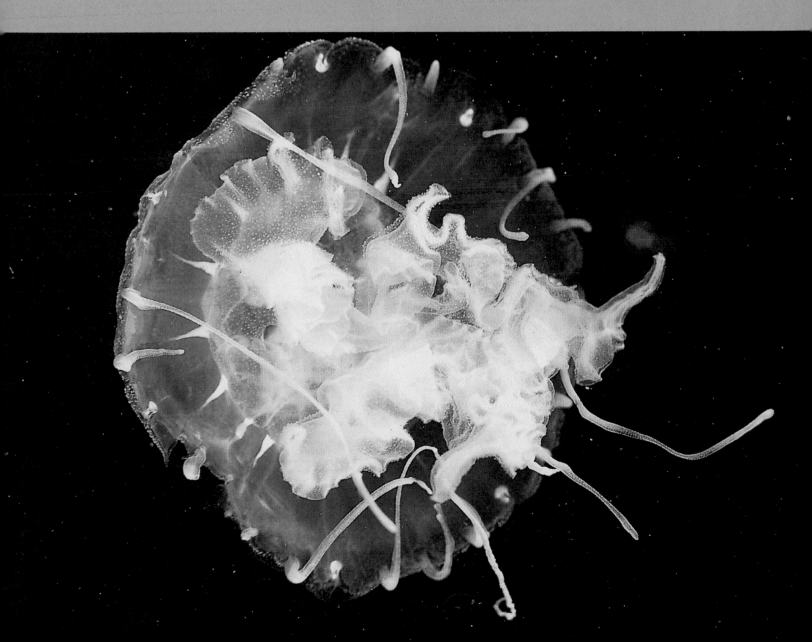

anemones and corals are also members of this group. Cnidarians have only two layers of cells—an inner and an outer layer—with a jellylike material in between.

A jellyfish has no brain. It has a set of very simple nerves and muscles. It drifts and swims along with the water currents, capturing small fish and other animals that get caught in its tentacles. The jellyfish's mouth is in the underside of its bell—the large blob of jelly that forms the top of the animal.

The body of a jellyfish may be simple, but its life cycle isn't. Sea nettles go through a complicated series of stages. These stages alternate between sexual and asexual reproduction.

A sea nettle begins life in mid- to late summer as a fertilized egg floating in the water of a bay or tidal river. The egg quickly hatches into a tiny swimming larva. The larva swims by moving the hairlike cilia that cover its body. It feeds on microscopic creatures in the water. After several days the larva swims to the bottom and attaches itself to a solid surface. Sea nettles usually attach themselves to the undersides of hard objects like oyster shells.

*These polyps will soon transform themselves into strobila. Each strobila will in turn generate five or more jellyfish.*

Once attached, the larva grows into a polyp. The polyp looks like a small, pink sea anemone. It grows tentacles and feeds on tiny creatures that swim into reach. Sea nettle polyps survive only in areas where the water is brackish.

As winter approaches and the water gets cold, some polyps may form a cyst—a dormant or resting stage. When the water warms again, the cyst regrows as a polyp. Others live through the entire winter in the polyp form. A mature polyp is about 1/2 inch (13 millimeters) long.

The polyp begins to reproduce by budding in late spring. At this stage it is called a strobila. The strobila looks like a tiny stack of dishes. One by one, the little jellyfish grow tentacles, separate themselves from the strobila, and float away. Polyps finish budding by late summer.

One strobila produces five or more little jellyfish. Each little jellyfish is an identical twin of the others. They are about 1/8 inch (3 millimeters) across. A polyp may live for several years, producing new jellyfish each spring.

The young sea nettles grow rapidly. They reach maturity as sexually reproducing adults in about a month. The adult stage—the one we usually call a jellyfish—is known as a medusa. Because of their long stinging tentacles, scientists named these creatures after the snake-haired monster of Greek mythology.

Looking from above, you can see a cloverleaf-shaped pattern at the top of the medusa. These are the reproductive organs. Medusae (plural) are either male or female. In mid- to late summer, the mature male medusae release sperm into the warm waters. The sperm enter the body cavity of females along with the water that flows in and out of the animals. Female medusae then release their eggs into their body cavity. The sperm fertilize the eggs. Then they drift out into the open water. With that, the life cycle of the sea nettle begins again.

Sea nettle medusae don't survive once the water begins to cool. By early fall the bay is free of jellyfish. But the next generation of little polyps is already hidden away and growing.

*This picture of a moon jellyfish clearly shows the cloverleaf-shaped reproductive organs of an adult, or medusa.*

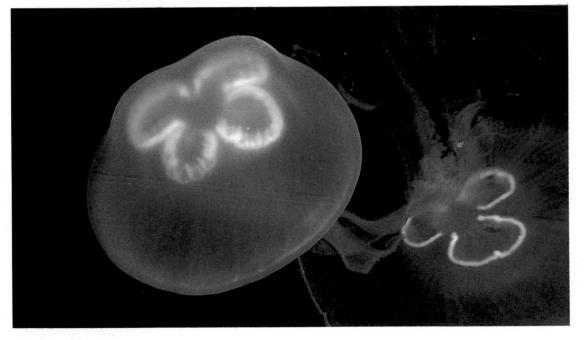

*b*ullfrogs are the largest frogs in North America. A full-grown bullfrog with its legs stretched behind it can be 18 inches (about 45 centimeters) long. Bullfrogs may live for up to fifteen years.

The bullfrog is an amphibian. The word "amphibian" comes from Greek words meaning "two lives." Amphibians begin their lives as fishlike creatures that breathe through gills. As they grow, their bodies change into air-breathing adults with lungs. Like most amphibians, bullfrogs need a watery environment to complete their life cycle.

Bullfrogs lay their eggs in lakes, ponds, and quiet pools in slow-moving streams. In the southern United States, the breeding season may begin as early as April. In the northern United States and Canada, bullfrogs don't lay their eggs until July. Bullfrog eggs are clear. In the center of each is a tiny black speck. That speck is the embryo that will eventually become a new frog.

*The bullfrog is a common sight in the lakes and streams of North America.*

# Bullfrog

## *Rana catesbeiana*

*Bullfrogs spend more than a year as tadpoles. These tadpoles will soon grow hind legs and be on their way to becoming an adult bullfrog.*

The frog eggs stick together in large, jellylike masses clinging to underwater plants in the shallow water.

After about ten days the embryo has developed into a larva, or tadpole. The tadpole wiggles out of the jelly coating its egg. Tadpoles breathe with gills, just as fish do. They swim in the shallow water and feed on algae and plants. As they grow older, tadpoles also eat dead animals that sink to the bottom of the pond. They even hunt for small animals swimming in the water.

Many frogs develop from egg to adult in just a couple of months. But bullfrogs take much longer. The bullfrog spends its first full year of life as a tadpole. By its second summer, the bullfrog tadpole is about 6 inches (15 centimeters) long. It then begins its metamorphosis into an adult frog.

Tiny hind legs begin to grow at the base of the tadpole's tail. As the legs grow larger, the tadpole's tail gradually disappears. The tadpole also loses its gills and develops lungs. It must now come to the surface of the pond to breathe air.

At the climax of metamorphosis, the new frog's front legs appear. Its skin toughens and its mouth and head change to the familiar frog shape. When metamorphosis is finished, the 6-inch tadpole has turned into a frog 2 inches (5 centimeters) long.

Bullfrogs are predators. They eat insects, fish, snakes, small mammals, other frogs, and almost anything else they can catch. The new frog spends the rest of the summer and fall hunting, mostly at night.

Each fall, bullfrogs bury themselves in the mud to hibernate through the cold winter months. When temperatures begin to warm in early spring, the bullfrogs emerge from hibernation and begin to hunt again.

A bullfrog is sexually mature two to four years after changing from a tadpole. Late in the spring, the mature males begin their mating calls. The bullfrog makes a loud, deep sound, using an expanding air sack under his jaw. The mating call can be heard for a quarter mile or more.

Each male bullfrog defends a territory in the pond from other males. His calls attract females to enter his territory and mate. The female releases her eggs into the water and the male fertilizes them with sperm. A female bullfrog may produce as many as 20,000 eggs, but only a few will survive and grow to become adult frogs.

The female leaves as soon as she has laid her eggs. The male keeps calling and guarding his territory. He may mate with several other females. Meanwhile, the newly laid eggs begin to grow into the next generation of bullfrogs.

*t*he female monarch butterfly is very choosy. She lays her eggs only on the tender new growth of a milkweed plant. Milkweed and a few similar plants are the only foods her offspring will eat. Altogether, a female monarch lays about 400 eggs. Once she has finished depositing her eggs, she dies.

The light-green egg develops into a tiny larva—a caterpillar—in about three days. The caterpillar chews its way out of its egg, and then eats it. The egg case is a good source of protein. The caterpillar then begins feeding on the milkweed leaves.

Like all insects, monarch caterpillars have no bones. A stiff outer skin, called an exoskeleton, supports its body. After a few days, the caterpillar has outgrown its skin. It must molt, or shed its skin, and grow a new one. It spins a

*Hundreds of thousands of monarch butterflies blanket the trees and fill the air at this resting site in Mexico. They have migrated here from the north to spend the winter.*

# Monarch Butterfly

## *Danaus plexippus*

thin, strong thread of silk from spinnerets at the rear of its body. Then, it grasps the silk with its legs and pulls itself out of its old skin. Molting requires a lot of effort. After it emerges, the caterpillar rests for several hours while its new, larger skin hardens. Then it starts to feed and grow again.

Each new larval form is called an instar. In two weeks, the caterpillars go through four different instars, growing larger and more colorful with each molt. A monarch larva in its final instar is brightly striped with yellow-green, black, and white rings. Birds don't like the taste of monarch caterpillars. The bright color warns them to leave the caterpillar alone.

When the larva reaches its full size—about 2 inches (5 centimeters)—it begins its transformation into adult form. Powerful chemical changes take place beneath the caterpillar's skin. It finds a sturdy leaf and weaves a button of silk on the underside. Grasping the leaf with its rear legs, the larva molts once more. But this time, what emerges from the old skin is not a caterpillar at all.

The monarch is now a pupa. The pupa attaches itself to the button of silk with tiny hooks at the end of its body. Then it hangs motionless for ten days inside a green shell called a chrysalis.

From outside the chrysalis, nothing seems to be happening. But inside, the monarch is changing dramatically. The pupa absorbs its juvenile organs like the large stomach and false legs. Adult organs grow— wings and wing muscles, long, thin legs, new mouthparts, and mature reproductive organs.

After ten days, the chrysalis cracks open and an adult monarch butterfly forces its way out. The butterfly clings to its chrysalis, while its heart pumps blood into its wings to stiffen them. Only then can it take flight. An adult monarch has a wingspan of up to 4 inches (10 centimeters).

The adult monarch does not eat. It only drinks nectar from flowers with its long, hollow tongue. The butterfly sends out powerful scents from special glands to attract a mate. When a male and female find each other, they fly together briefly. Then they mate. The actual mating lasts for several hours. The male has a small penis at the end of his abdomen. He deposits a waxy packet of sperm into the female's reproductive opening. The female then flies off to lay her eggs. The male may mate with several different females before he dies.

During the summer, monarchs go through this cycle three or four times. The butterflies move northward, following their food supply. When fall comes, the season's last butterflies make an amazing journey. The butterflies gather in large groups. They fly south to winter resting sites in the southern United States, Mexico, and the Caribbean. Male monarchs lead the migration. Scientists think they mark the way with special scent glands.

*From the outside, not much appears to be happening in this chrysalis. But the changes taking place inside are some of the most dramatic in nature.*

What's most amazing is that the migrating butterflies were born in the northern United States and Canada. They have never been in the South. But somehow they find their way to their winter homes. Some monarchs fly up to 2,000 miles (3,200 kilometers) in this migration. It's a tremendous flight for such a small animal.

The monarchs gather by the hundreds of thousands at their winter homes. They rest on trees, sometimes covering them like black and golden leaves.

Many butterflies don't survive the long flight or the winter temperatures. But when the sun warms the butterflies the following spring, the survivors fly northward. They mate and lay the eggs that renew this cycle for another year.

*It is hard to believe that this large, colorful monarch butterfly emerged from a chrysalis just like the one below it, where it was transformed from a caterpillar.*

*t*he word that best describes the opossum is "adaptable." Opossums eat fruit, berries, corn, worms, insects, frogs, eggs, birds, and almost anything else. Opossums are most active at night. They are both hunters and scavengers. They are good swimmers and excellent climbers.

Opossums have adapted to living near humans, too. They often raid people's gardens, trash cans, and chicken coops. They nest in burrows, in hollow trees, under fallen logs, or under houses. Opossums live as far north as Canada, and as far south as Argentina.

An opossum is about the size of a house cat. It has a pointy snout, beady black eyes, sharp teeth, and a hairless tail. It uses the tail for grasping things. An opossum lines its nest with dry leaves that it carries home with its tail.

*Although too large to fit in their mother's pouch, these baby opossums will cling to her and ride on her back until they are old enough to take care of themselves.*

# Opossum

*Didelphis virginiana*

Opossums belong to a group of mammals called marsupials. Marsupials rear their young in pouches on their bellies. Only females have pouches. Marsupials are very common in Australia—kangaroos, koalas, and wallabies are all marsupials. But in the rest of the world, marsupials are very unusual. The opossum is the only marsupial native to North America.

Mammal embryos develop inside the mother's body, in an organ called the uterus. Most female mammals have a lining in the uterus—called the placenta. The placenta is supplied with blood that nourishes the growing embryos. The embryos spend a long time attached to their mother's placenta by an umbilical cord. Raccoon embryos take about 60 days to develop, for example. Cat embryos spend 65 days in their mother's uterus.

The development of marsupial embryos is very different. Female marsupials don't have a placenta to keep the growing embryos fed. So marsupial embryos must be born very quickly. An opossum begins life as a fertilized egg in its mother's uterus and is born only 13 days after fertilization.

When it's born, an opossum weighs less than a tenth of an ounce (about 2 grams). It is smaller than a pea. As the mother opossum gives birth, she props herself up on her hind legs, so that the pouch is higher than the birth canal. The tiny, hairless babies have sharp nails on their well-developed front legs. The rear legs are hardly developed at all. The babies climb through their mother's fur to her pouch. They must travel about 3 inches (7.5 centimeters)—a very long journey for such tiny creatures. The mother wets the hair between her birth canal and the opening to her pouch with her tongue to make it easier for the babies to make the trip. The nails fall off the babies' paws soon after they reach the pouch.

The babies crawl into the pouch and attach themselves to one of the mother's nipples. Like other mammals, opossums feed their young with milk. When a baby starts nursing, the nipple swells and holds the tiny opossum in place. A female opossum has about eleven nipples. The average litter is about 9, but she may give birth to 20 babies or more. Any baby that does not find a nipple will not survive.

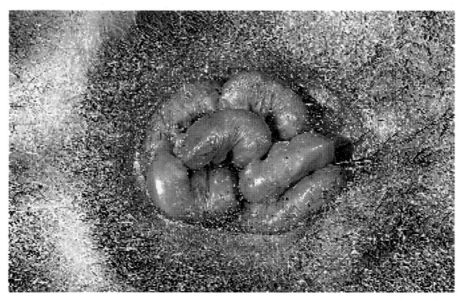

*Just fifteen days old, these opossum babies have completed the journey to their mother's pouch, where they will stay until they are fully developed.*

*These eight-week old oppossum babies are just beginning to grow hair.*

The babies nurse in their mother's pouch for about 60 days. By the end of the first month, they are the size of mice and have started growing fur. After two months, they begin leaving the pouch. The babies ride on their mother's back, clinging to her fur with their tails. After three months they have stopped nursing and eat only solid food. The young opossums still cling to their mother's back for several weeks. Then they are ready to begin life on their own.

Opossums are solitary animals—they live by themselves. The young opossums wander off to hunt, feed, and grow. Opossums don't hibernate during the winter, but they spend much of their time curled up in their nests.

In late winter, the opossums—now adults—are ready to mate. As with other mammals, opossum eggs are fertilized inside the mother's body. When they mate, the male opossum deposits his sperm inside the female's birth canal with his penis. The sperm swim through the uterus toward the ovaries, to fertilize the eggs. The opossum's life cycle begins again, with a new generation of tiny embryos.

Male and female opossums don't stay together after mating. The female raises her litter of babies on her own. A mother opossum will often raise two litters during the spring and summer breeding season. Most opossums don't survive for more than two or three years in the wild.

*a*lthough they might not look like it, seahorses are fish. Like other fish, they have a skeleton, gills, and small fins. Instead of fishlike scales, seahorses are covered with hard, bony plates.

Seahorses live in warm shallow waters, where there is plenty of seaweed or sea grasses. They cling to the underwater plants with their flexible tails. Many seahorses change color to blend with their surroundings. This camouflage protects them from predators, and hides them as they wait among the plants for their prey. When a small animal swims by, they snap their jaws open with a clicking sound and suck the prey into their mouths.

Seahorses are not very large. The biggest seahorse grows to a length of about 18 inches (45 centimeters). Most of the many known species are much smaller. Scientists fear that seahorses are being overfished in some parts of

*Seahorses are fascinating and beautiful creatures. There are many different species, but most of them share very similar life cycles.*

# Seahorse

*Hippocampus erectus*
and other species

the world. Dried seahorses are used as decoration. People in some Asian countries also use dried seahorse as an ingredient in medicines. Pollution of the sea-grass beds where these animals live has also hurt seahorse populations.

Seahorses are unique creatures. What's most special about them is their remarkable life cycle. Seahorse males give birth! The adult male has a pouch below its belly where baby seahorses develop and grow.

Like the males of many other animals, male seahorses compete with one another for available females. A pair of seahorses stays together through the entire summer breeding season. When adult seahorses mate, the male and female do a mating dance. Then, anchoring themselves with their tails, the two animals cling together belly to belly.

The female places 150 to 200 eggs into the pouch of the male with a tube called an ovipositor. The female's part in raising the young is then finished. The male fertilizes the eggs with sperm released inside the pouch.

The eggs attach themselves to the lining of the male's pouch. The lining of the pouch does much the same job as the placenta that lines the uterus of female mammals. The eggs receive oxygen and food from the male's blood as they develop. The pouch gets bigger and bigger as the young seahorses grow inside.

The female visits the male regularly each day. They greet each other by changing colors, linking tails, and swimming together. Then the female goes off to feed.

Finally, after several weeks (the exact time depends on the species), the male seahorse pushes the babies out of his pouch. He releases the babies in groups over several days. Sometimes he pushes against rocks or other hard objects to help squeeze the babies out.

The baby seahorses look like tiny miniatures of their parents. The babies swim around their father for a little while. Then they seek shelter from predators In the nearby grasses. They swim in a horizontal position like ordinary fish for a few days. Then they swim in an upright position, like their parents.

Soon after the male gives birth, the female is ready to deposit more eggs in his pouch. A male seahorse stays pregnant throughout the breeding season. Seahorses may live as long as three to four years in an aquarium, but most don't survive that long in the wild. Seahorses grow to full size in about five months. They are then ready to find mates and begin the cycle again.

*Anchoring himself to a nearby plant, a male seahorse gives birth. More baby seahorses will be born over the next several days.*

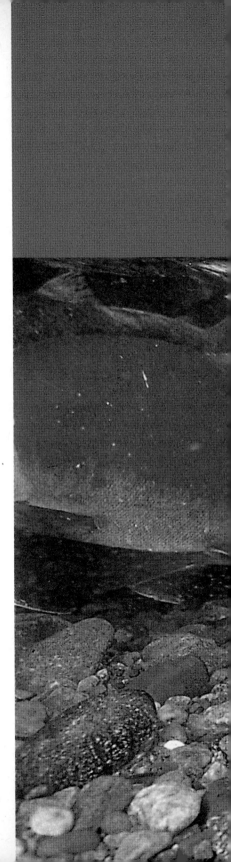

*a* sockeye salmon starts life as a pink egg in a cold, clear stream in the Pacific Northwest—anywhere from northern California to Alaska. Salmon eggs are buried 6 to 9 inches (15 to 23 centimeters) deep in the gravel of the stream. Each egg measures about 1/4 inch (6 millimeters) across.

Eggs take from 50 to 140 days to hatch, depending on the temperature of the water. Salmon usually lay their eggs in the late summer or fall. The eggs hatch the following spring.

Salmon fishing is very important to the economy of the Pacific Northwest, so scientists and fishermen know the salmon's life cycle well; they have names for all the salmon's different life stages. When the eggs hatch, the young salmon are called "alevins." The alevins spend their first month hiding from predators in the gravel. They survive on the nutrition stored in yolk sacs attached to their bellies.

*Ready to spawn, adult sockeye salmon swim up a northern stream. After spawning, the salmon's life is over.*

# Sockeye Salmon

## *Oncorhynchus nerka*

*Salmon emerge from their eggs as alevins, which can be seen at the left of the picture. They feed on the yolk sac attached to them until it is used up.*

After about three to five weeks, the alevins have used up their yolk sacs. The young salmon—now known as "fry"—must swim in search of food. Fry hunt at night. They spend their days hiding under rocks, leaves, or fallen branches on the stream bottom.

Sockeye salmon spend most of their young lives in lakes. The fry follow the stream to a nearby lake that is part of the river system. There they feed on small crustaceans and insects, and hide from predators. In their second year, young salmon are called "fingerlings" or "parr."

When they are about 4 inches (10 centimeters) long—usually after two years in the lake—the fingerlings begin to change. They've lived their entire lives in fresh water. But now they develop the ability to live in salt water. The silvery young salmon—now called "smolts"—migrate downstream to the Pacific Ocean.

*As smolts, these young salmon migrate down an Alaskan river toward the Pacific Ocean. They will spend the next few years feeding and growing in the salty waters of the North Pacific.*

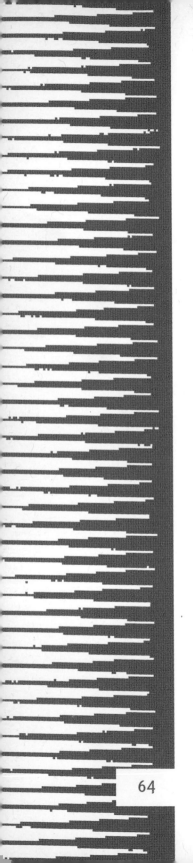

Only about 5 percent of the salmon that hatched two years earlier have survived to make this trip, and the migration takes a heavy toll on the remaining fish. Predators wait to feed on the smolts; tumbling water, dams, and other obstructions kill many others.

In the ocean, sockeye salmon spend about three years feeding on crustaceans, squid, and smaller fish. Salmon are strong, speedy swimmers. An adult can swim as fast as 14 miles (22 kilometers) per hour. Adult sockeyes grow to over 2 feet (0.6 meter) long. They can weigh as much as 15 pounds (6.8 kilograms), but most weigh no more than 8 pounds (3.6 kilograms).

The mature salmon begin a long, difficult journey back to their home streams to spawn. As they migrate, their bodies change again. Males develop a red color, with green fins. They grow a large, hooked jaw and a humped back. Females also change in color and shape, but not quite so dramatically.

The Pacific Ocean is huge. But somehow, the salmon manage to find their home rivers. Once they enter fresh water, the fish stop eating. As the fish struggle upstream, many predators wait for them. Eagles, seals, ospreys, bears, and humans catch and eat many of the returning salmon. Scavengers like foxes, raccoons, and ravens feast on the sockeyes that aren't strong enough to complete the journey.

The salmon that reach their home streams are ready to spawn. The female rolls back and forth. She digs a nest 6 to 12 inches (15 to 30 centimeters) deep in the gravel of the streambed.  Meanwhile, male salmon fight one another for the chance to mate with the female. The winning male keeps guard while the female completes her nest. Finally, the female lays her eggs in the nest and the male releases his sperm over them. The female covers the fertilized eggs with gravel. She may dig several nests and mate with different males. Altogether, she produces up to 3,500 eggs. Fewer than one in a thousand of those eggs will survive to complete the life cycle as a reproducing adult.

Once the salmon have spawned, their lives are over. Within a few days, sockeye and other Pacific salmon die in the stream where they were born. Scavengers feast on their remains.

Salmon are very important in the food web of the Pacific Northwest. Many other animals rely on them for food. The decaying salmon fertilize the rivers and nearby land. Unfortunately, overfishing, damming of rivers, and water pollution now threaten the salmon's life cycle in many parts of the Northwest.

n animal like a bullfrog or a salmon is considered a predator. It hunts and kills other animals for food. But other animals feed on an animal or plant slowly, without killing it. These organisms are called parasites. The organism they feed on is called the host.

Sometimes the parasite causes the host very little harm. A tick, for example, attaches itself to the skin of a mammal, sucks some of its blood, and then drops away. Unless the tick carries a disease, the mammal easily replaces the little blood it lost. But other parasites can cause enough damage to eventually kill the host.

Parasites are very common in nature. Most animals and plants serve as hosts to many different parasites. Humans, too, can be hosts. One of the most harmful human parasites is the blood fluke or schistosome.

*The thicker, bluish blood fluke is the male. The dark area in the thinner and lighter-colored female is the half-digested blood from a recent meal.*

# Blood Fluke

## *Schistosoma mansoni*

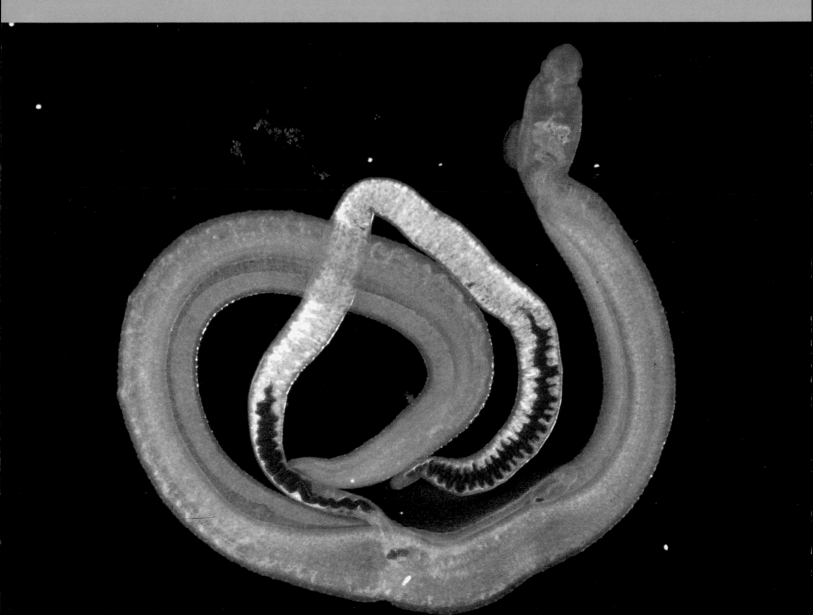

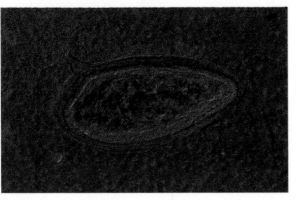

*This blood fluke egg will next become a swimming larva that will burrow into a snail—the first host it will need to continue its life cycle.*

The blood fluke needs two different hosts—a snail and a human—to complete its life cycle. A blood fluke begins life as a fertilized egg in the intestine of a human. It travels through the blood to the lower intestine. The egg has a spine. It burrows its way through the wall of the intestine and then leaves in the host's feces, or intestinal waste. Another species of blood fluke lives in the bladder. Its eggs pass out of the body with urine. Blood flukes live where human sanitation is poor, or where farmers use human wastes to fertilize their fields.

The egg must reach water to complete the next stage in its life cycle. When it reaches water, the egg hatches into a swimming larva. The larva searches for a freshwater snail. When it finds one, it burrows into the skin of the snail. Larvae that don't find a snail host die within 24 hours.

The larvae then metamorphose into a reproductive form, called a sporocyst. The sporocyst reproduces asexually. Over six or seven weeks, it produces hundreds of microscopic swimming larvae. These tiny larvae are very different from the larva that first infected the snail. They leave the snail and swim in search of a new human host. If a pond or stream has the right kind of snails living in it, anyone wading or washing will probably be infected.

When they touch human skin, the larvae attach themselves with a gluelike substance. They produce chemicals that soften the skin. Then they bore their way into a blood vessel. Later, the place where a larva entered the skin will have an itchy rash. But by that time, the fluke has already entered the person's blood.

The larvae travel through the bloodstream. They have suckers on their mouths and bellies. Those that reach the blood vessels of the intestine attach themselves to the vessel walls. The flukes feed on their host's blood and grow into mature adult forms.

Adult blood flukes are either male or female. A male blood fluke may be up to $3/8$ of an inch (1 centimeter) long. Females are smaller and thinner. The larger male folds himself around a female. The female begins producing eggs, which the male fertilizes, starting this complicated life cycle once again. Females may produce 500 or more eggs a day. Adult blood flukes may survive for 25 years, if their hosts live that long.

Infection with blood flukes causes a disease called schistosomiasis. The disease causes pain and weakness and damages internal organs. Unless people infected with schistosomiasis are treated with drugs, they release schistosome eggs into their environment every day.

Schistosomiasis is a worldwide health problem—it affects hundreds of thousands of people. So far, efforts to control the spread of the disease have not been very successful. Doctors can treat the disease if they discover it early enough. Improved sanitation can help control the disease. But scientists are still searching for a way to kill the host snails without killing fish and other wildlife.

# afterword

The earth has a huge number of species. Scientists still don't know how many millions of different kinds of animals, plants, and other creatures populate our planet. These species have great variety in their life cycles. The twelve animals in this book are just a tiny example of that amazing variety.

But even more amazing is how much we all have in common. Most animals have similar body parts and similar body functions. We all gather food, digest it, and use it to fuel our activities. We absorb oxygen and give off carbon dioxide. Most animals have a heart and blood system to carry the oxygen and food to our cells. Most have nerves to gather and carry information. We have muscles so that we can move, and skin to protect us from the outside world. The list of similarities goes on and on.

We are all made of cells that perform many similar, specialized tasks. When scientists study cells more closely, they find even more similarities. Almost all of the earth's creatures carry the information they need to grow and reproduce in the very same way: Humans, and all the other animals you've read about, use large molecules of DNA (deoxyribonucleic acid) to store and pass on this information.

Human DNA and the DNA of a penguin, a seahorse, or an opossum are very much alike. All creatures are connected as part of the long history of life on earth.

Each species, and each individual creature, is part of a great web of life. The life of each species—including our own—depends on the lives of many others. Plants produce the oxygen we need to breathe. Insects and birds pollinate the plants we depend on for food. Insects, worms, and bacteria help decompose the wastes we produce.

Human beings cannot survive without the other animals and plants, fungi, and bacteria in the web of life. Unless we care for and preserve these other creatures, our own lives are in danger.

To preserve life on earth, the first step is to understand it. We must learn how other species live, and what they need to grow and reproduce. Other creatures that share our planet may seem very different from us. But we must learn to appreciate, respect, and understand those differences. Otherwise, our human activities could interrupt the life cycles of those other creatures, and they could be lost from earth forever.

# glossary

*Abdomen*: the rearmost section of an insect's or crustacean's body.

*Adult*: a fully grown, mature organism able to reproduce.

*Amphibian*: a class of animals with backbones that begin life in water and later live on land. Amphibians include frogs, toads, and salamanders.

*Asexual reproduction*: the creation of offspring without the joining of male and female cells.

*Budding*: a type of asexual reproduction. In budding, offspring are produced as outgrowths from a parent organism.

*Chrysalis*: the pupa stage in the life cycle of a moth or butterfly; or, the outer covering for that stage.

*Cilia*: hairlike organs that a tiny organism uses to propel itself through water.

*Clitellum*: the broad, lighter-colored band near the front end of an earthworm.

*Cloaca*: a single opening in the rear of many animals. The cloaca is used both to get rid of body wastes and as an entrance and exit of the reproductive system.

*Cnidarians*: a group of jellylike animals including jellyfish, sea anemones, and hydroids.

*Crèche*: a tight cluster of young penguins—from the French word for "crib."

*Crustacean*: a class of animals with jointed legs and stiff exoskeletons, including shrimp, crabs, daphnia, and many others. Most crustaceans live in water.

*Cyst*: the rounded body form that some animals take during a resting stage of their life cycle.

*Diversity*: variety.

*Dormant*: resting or sleeping.

*Dorsal*: referring to the back or upper side of an animal.

*Egg*: the female reproductive cell.

*Embryo*: an organism in its earliest stages of growth, shortly after fertilization.

*Exoskeleton*: the hard outer covering of many animals.

*Fertilization*: the joining of sperm and egg cells to begin the process of reproduction.

*Genes*: units of information in every cell that tell an organism how to develop and grow. Genes are passed on from parent to offspring in reproduction.

*Hermaphrodite*: an organism with both male and female reproductive organs.

*Host*: any organism that provides nourishment and shelter for a parasite.

*Incubation*: the period it takes an egg to develop before it hatches.

*Instar*: a stage between molts of an insect.

*Juvenile*: a young or immature organism; one not yet ready to reproduce.

*Larva*: a juvenile stage in the life cycle of many animals. Larvae are able to get their own food and survive independently.

*Marsupial*: a mammal that carries its young in a pouch.

*Medusa*: the mature reproductive stage in the life cycle of some cnidarians. Medusae are commonly known as jellyfish.

*Metamorphosis*: a rapid change in body form.

*Molt*: to shed an exoskeleton or other outer body covering.

*Offspring*: the new creatures that are created by reproduction.

*Organism*: a living being.

*Ovipositor*: an egg-laying tube found in the female of many insects and other animals.

*Parasite*: an organism that lives in or on another species, and gets nutrients and shelter from it.

*Parent*: an adult organism that has produced offspring.

*Parthenogenesis*: the growth of unfertilized eggs to produce offspring.

*Penis*: a male reproductive organ used to place sperm into the female's reproductive organs.

*Placenta*: an organ that nourishes developing embryos in the uterus of most female mammals.

*Polyp*: a stage in the life cycle of a cnidarian. A polyp is a hollow, tube-shaped body attached to a solid surface.

*Predator*: an animal that catches and kills other animals for food.

*Pupa*: a resting, nonfeeding stage in the life cycle of many insects.

*Reproduction*: the process by which organisms make more members of their species.

*Schistosome*: a blood fluke; one of a family of parasitic flatworms.

*Schistosomiasis*: the human disease caused by infection with schistosomes.

*Sexual reproduction*: the creation of offspring by joining male and female reproductive cells (sperm and egg).

*Spawn*: to produce eggs and sperm; this word is usually applied to aquatic animals.

*Species*: a single, distinct group of animals or plants that share common characteristics. Members of a species generally reproduce only among themselves.

*Sperm*: the male reproductive cell.

*Sporocyst*: an stage in the life cycle of schistosomes and some other animals, during which the animal reproduces asexually.

*Sterile*: unable to reproduce.

*Strobila*: a stage in the life cycle of cnidarians and other animals. Offspring are produced as buds from one end of the strobila.

*Umbilical cord*: the vessel that carries blood and nourishment between the embryo of a mammal and its mother's placenta.

*Uterus*: the part of a female mammal's reproductive system in which embryos develop.

*Ventral*: referring to the lower or underside of an animal.

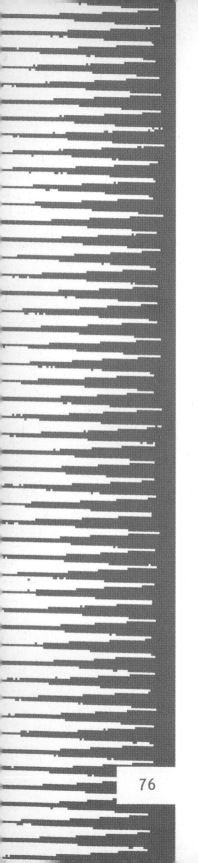

# *further reading*

Benedict, Kitty. *The Earthworm*. Mankato, MN: Creative Education, 1992.

Cone, Molly. *Come Back, Salmon: How a Group of Dedicated Kids Adopted Pigeon Creek and Brought It Back to Life*. San Francisco: Sierra Club, 1992.

Facklam, Howard and Margery. *Parasites*. New York: 21st Century Books, 1994.

Gowell, Elizabeth T. *Sea Jellies: Rainbows in the Sea*. Danbury, CT: Franklin Watts, 1993.

Hunt, Joni P. *Butterflies: Monarchs, Moths and More—Up Close and Unexpected*. Morristown, NJ: Silver Burdett, 1994.

Marko, Katherine M. *Pocket Babies*. Danbury, CT: Franklin Watts, 1995.

Parker, Steve. *Frogs and Toads*. San Francisco: Sierra Club, 1994.

Parramon, J.M. *The Fascinating World of Bees*. Hauppauge, NY: Barron's, 1991.

Pohl, Kathleen. *Crabs*. Chatham, NJ: Raintree Steck-Vaughn, 1986.

Schlein, Miriam. *The Dangerous Life of the Seahorse*. New York: Atheneum, 1986.

Sømme, Lauritz and Kalas, Sybille. *The Penguin Family Book*. New York: North-South Books, 1995.

# index